Self-Help Books for Women

Dr. Robertino Bedenian

Published by Dr. Robertino Bedenian, 2024.

SELF-HELP BOOKS FOR WOMEN

First edition. January 14, 2024.

Copyright © 2024 Dr. Robertino Bedenian.

ISBN: 979-8224217717

Written by Dr. Robertino Bedenian.

Also by Dr. Robertino Bedenian

Fitness Over 60 For Women – How to Stay Fit And Healthy As You Age

Does Back Pain Go Away? 10 Answers To The Most Acute Back Pain Issues

Massage Bible - A Beginners Guide To Western And Eastern Massage Therapy

Going Vegan - How To Vegan Without Going Crazy

Chiropraktik - Was Steckt Eigentlich Dahinter?

Massagen: Ein Überblick Über Westliche Und Östliche Massagetechniken

Natuerlich Abnehmen, Schlank Und Endlich Fit Sein

P.S. Ich Liebe Dich: Wenn Liebe So Einfach Wäre

Was Tun Bei Rückenschmerzen, Bandscheibenvorfall Und Ischiasschmerzen: 10 Antworten Zu Den Häufigsten Fragen Bei Rückenschmerzen

Was Tun Gegen Schlafapnoe, Schlafstörungen Und Schnarchen

Self-Help Books for Women

Diabetes How to Help: Everything You Need to Know About Diabetes Type 1 and Type 2

Diet and Workout Planner: How to Stay Healthy and Get Fit for Life

Everything I Know About Love

The Sleep Easy Solution Book: How to Stop Sleep Apnea, Snoring, and Sleep Disorders

Your Super Gut Feeling Restored – How to Restore Your Life Energy and Overall Health from The Inside Out

Watch for more at https://booksummarypublishing.com.

Table of Contents

Chapter 1:Introduction to Self-Help for Women 1

Chapter 2: Self-Help in Mental Health 9

Chapter 3: Self-Help for Women in Depression and Anxiety 18

Chapter 4: Self-Help for Women in Divorce 24

Chapter 5: Self-Help in Health 30

Chapter 6: Self-Help in Trauma 38

Chapter 7: Self-Help For Dependents 47

Chapter 8: Self-Help in Career for Women 56

Chapter 9: Self-Help for Happiness for Women 68

Chapter 10: Self-Help for Spiritual Care 76

Self-Help Books for Women

How to Overcome Depression, Anxiety, Divorce, and Trauma

By

Dr. Robertino Bedenian

Chapter 1: Introduction to Self-Help for Women

What is Self-Help?

The act or process of self-betterment or resolving one's issues (emotionally, economically, or psychologically without the help of others.

<u>Or</u>

Coping with one's personal or emotional difficulties without the assistance of a professional.

What is Psychological Self-Help?

Psychological self-help involves learning how to help yourself and then using what you've learned to have long-term positive change. Advice is available in a variety of formats, covering a wide range of issues from money to self-help, to personal success, and mental illness.

Why Self-Help is Important!

Self-care does not mean that you are choosing yourself above a loved one. It simply means that you are being aware of your own needs which is a prior condition so you can help others you care about. You are best prepared to fulfill the requirements of others when you take care of yourself and are not stressed.

There are several types of self-care. Self-care itself is not complex; it can be as easy as taking a deep breath when you feel you are becoming tired. Maintaining your physical and emotional health will likely leave you better off to deal with the pressures that come with caring for someone you love.

Why Self-Help Is Important for Women!

Women must prioritize self-help. Follow these self-care techniques to help you care for yourself and achieve life balance. Keep in your mind that self-help doesn't mean you are selfish. When women do not prioritize self-care, they frequently feel like victims of something outside of themselves, with limits and limitations. This inhibits women from having a fulfilling and happy life.

Strategies for Self-Help

For women, emotional, mental, and physical well-being self-help is very crucial. You shouldn't neglect the importance of self-help.

Recognize Your Worth

Self-help is important for maintaining a healthy relationship with yourself since it develops happy feelings and improves confidence and self-esteem. Self-help is also important for reminding yourself and others that you and your needs are important.

Create Support Surrounding

Take a look around. Do your surroundings inspire you, or do they make you feel anxious and messy? Create a supportive environment by eliminating the clutter of the things that exhaust you. Get rid of the clutter in your house, vehicle, and office. Remove clutter from connections as well, such as one-sided interactions. Find companions that want to improve their lives as well. This way, you can encourage each other and also be a role model for those around you. It will also support you in balancing the many responsibilities you play as a woman.

Be Your Sincere Friend

What if you treated yourself the same way you would treat your best friend? You would most likely be more aware of your own needs, issues, and priorities. You would be as kind to yourself as you are to others. You would appreciate and preserve your health and well-being. You would put all others aside to be your friend. Taking care of your health is one of the most important things you can do for your family and friends. You can begin now by being a loyal person to yourself!

Enjoy Your Me-Time

Spending quality time alone doesn't mean you are living a lonely life. Spending time alone allows the rest of the world to continue spinning while you relax, recharge, and refocus. Spending quality time alone can be as simple as sitting quietly outside, reading a book in the park, or relaxing in your favorite comfortable chair with a cup of tea.

Believe that it is OK to say "No"!

How many times have you said "yes," "fine," or "no problem" to a request, only to soon regret your choice? Have you ever devoted your energy, time, or money to a project although having little or no desire to participate? Saying no is a discipline, and it is an important self-care habit that may improve your confidence and release your inner strength.

Rewrite Your Methodology

Begin by putting your priorities into your daily routine. Allow others' priorities on your calendar once your priorities have been met. These changes may be seen by others in your life. Share your strategy with them, and explain why you need to take care of yourself. They will notice the benefits of self-care in your attitude and approach to life, as well as the direct benefit of being in a relationship with a more balanced you!

Stress Management:

Stress management: Smart self-care practices such as eating properly, interacting with a loved one, or yoga mindfulness help reduce the consequences of stress by improving your mood and boosting your energy and confidence.

Power of Self-Help for Women:

The self-help groups have been very effective in enabling women to develop their skills and confidence, as well as raise their incomes.

The groups provide both financial and social help, empowering people by providing them with a strong network of supporters. The projects' goals can be quite different: some have helped women in accumulating their savings, while others have targeted sexual violence, alcoholism, or social-related issues.

Benefits of Self-Help

Self-Help Is Empowering

Creating a self-help strategy puts you in charge of your future. The skills and strategies you gain while participating in the self-help process are likely to be useful to you in a variety of areas of your life. It is also emotionally satisfying to deal with problems on your own; it makes you feel like a responsible and capable adult.

A personalized strategy is what self-help involves:

Designing your self-help plan allows you to tailor your efforts to your strengths and weaknesses, as well as your personal preferences for how to effectively handle specific issues.

Self-Help Makes You A Better, Wiser Person

Self-help efforts can help you learn to identify prospective issues before they start (or at least early on in their course) so that you can head them off before they become serious by increasing your self-awareness capabilities. As your objectivity (the ability to see things as they are rather than how you want them to be) develops, you'll find yourself increasingly capable of being your own best therapist, guiding yourself away from bad judgments.

Self-Help Is Private

If you are a private person who feels uncomfortable discussing secrets with others, self-help can save you the embarrassment of expressing your issues and problems with another person.

Self-help is inexpensive and available

Self-help is typically free, and learning about it is either free or affordable. If you reside in a rural or small town, self-help may be one of the few viable alternatives for obtaining assistance.

Self-Help Is a Time Saver

Pursuing self-help efforts saves you the time you otherwise would spend with a therapist who could manage your difficulties.

Disadvantages of Self-Help

Lack of knowledge

Even if you can be objective and exact about the nature of your problems, figuring out how to resolve them is difficult. Creating a useful self-help plan needs proper knowledge: Understanding of what is causing your difficulties, and understanding of how those problems can be resolved. People are not born with the ability to solve issues.

Before you can decide the best techniques for assisting yourself, you should have access to resources and the motivation to read and study those resources. This task is not for everyone because not everyone is capable or willing to perform it.

Lack of motivation

There is one more problem: Even if you know what to do to fix an issue, you aren't always able to adhere to your strategy and follow through effectively enough to take advantage of the strategy. Creating and maintaining the motivation required to stay in a self-help strategy can be quite difficult. Even when confronted with uncomfortable situations that you desperately want to resolve, not every woman can adequately motivate and control herself.

Difficulty in understanding the problem

Your potential to help yourself will be constrained only by your ability to be objective and clear about the nature of your problems. It is extremely tough to figure out what your problems are on your own. You may not have enough objectivity and perspective in challenging times to make a fair and honest evaluation or conclusion about your issues. People find many ways to reject or distort the reality about what is wrong in their life, even when such denial approaches may not suit their long-term interests. For example, they make themselves so much busy in their work like workaholics. You can easily be in denial about your issues and using defense mechanisms to avoid getting aware of them or understanding their real nature. If this is the case, you will most likely become unable to realize the actual nature of your problems. Since you can't solve what you don't understand, you'll be unable to resolve your problems and may even worsen them if you try a self-help method.

Takeaway

Self-improvement is the act or process of improving oneself or addressing one's problems (emotionally, monetarily, or psychologically) without the assistance of others. Psychological self-help entails learning how to help yourself and then applying what you've learned to achieve long-term good results.

Self-care does not have to be difficult; it may be as simple as taking a deep breath when you feel exhausted.

Maintaining your physical and emotional health will make it easier for you to deal with the stresses of caring for someone you love.

Women must make self-care a priority. If you care for yourself and attain life balance, you can also use these self-care strategies to help others. Self-help is essential for establishing a good relationship with yourself since it fosters positive emotions and enhances self-esteem. You cannot live in peace with others if you don't live in peace with yourself.

Look for a partner who wants to improve her life as well. Both of you will benefit from mutual assistance, and you will be a role model for everyone around you. One of the most essential things you can do for your family and friends is to take care of your health. You may start right now by being faithful to yourself!

Sitting quietly outside, reading a book in the park, or relaxing in your favorite comfortable chair with a cup of tea can all be good ways to spend quality time alone. Explain why you need to take care of yourself and share your strategy with them. They'll notice the positive effects of self-care on your attitude and outlook on life, as well as the direct benefit of being in a relationship with someone who is more balanced!

Self-help groups have proven to be quite helpful in helping women improve their skills and confidence while also increasing their income. The skills and tactics you learn as part of the self-help process are likely to be useful in the future.

By enhancing your self-awareness capacities, self-help activities can help you learn to spot potential troubles before they start (or at least early in their course) so that you can head them off before they become serious. It might be challenging to develop and sustain the drive needed to stick with a self-help technique. Even when confronted with difficult situations that you sincerely want to overcome, not everyone can keep herself motivated and under control.

Chapter 2: Self-Help in Mental Health

What Is Mental Health?

Our emotional, psychological, and social well-being all contribute to our mental health. It influences how we think, feel, and act. It also affects how we deal with stress, interact with other people, and make decisions. Mental health is essential at all stages of life, from infancy through adolescence to maturity.

Factors Affecting Mental Health

If you have mental health issues during your life, your thinking, emotions, and behavior may be disturbed. Many factors contribute to mental health issues, including:

Genes and brain chemistry are examples of biological factors.

Trauma or abuse are examples of life experiences or environmental exposure.

There is an inherited trait of mental health issues.

Biological Factors

Neurotransmitters are brain chemicals that transmit signals to other parts of the brain and body. When these neurotransmitters' brain networks are affected, the function of nerve receptors and nerve systems changes, leading to depression and other emotional disorders.

Inherited Trait

People with a mental illness are more likely to have a blood relative with a mental disease. Certain genes may increase your risk of obtaining a mental disorder, while your life situation may accelerate it.

Life Experiences or Environmental Exposure

Environmental stress, inflammatory diseases, poisons, alcohol, or drugs can all be related to mental disorders while in the womb. Trauma or abuse also causes mental illness.

Signs and Symptoms

- Sad or depressed
- Thinking that is confused or has a decreased ability to focus
- Excessive anxieties or fears, or feelings of intense guilt
- Extreme mood swings (highs and lows)
- Withdrawal from social activities and friends
- Significant fatigue, poor energy, or sleeping difficulties
- Delusions, paranoia, or hallucinations are all examples of detachment from reality
- Experiencing unexplainable aches and pains
- Feeling helpless or miserable
- Excessive smoking, drinking, or drug use
- Having difficulty understanding and relating to issues and people
- Problems with alcohol or drug abuse
- Significant changes in dietary habits
- Changes in sexual desire
- Excessive anger, hatred, or violence
- Suicidal thoughts

Complications

Mental disease is a major source of disability. Untreated mental illness can result in serious emotional, behavioral, and physical health issues. Complications related to mental illness include:

- Unhappiness and a lack of delight in life
- Family disagreements
- Difficulties in relationships
- Problems with cigarettes, alcohol, and other drugs cause social isolation.
- Work or school missed, or other issues related to work or school
- A legal and financial issue
- Homelessness and poverty
- Self-injury and harm to others, including suicide or homicide
- Because of a weakened immune system, your body has a difficult time fighting infection.
- Cardiovascular disease and other medical conditions.

Treatment

Your treatment will be chosen by the type of mental illness you have, the severity of the disease, and what works best for you. In many cases, a combination of treatments is the most effective. Treatment from your health care physician may be adequate if you have a moderate mental disorder with well-controlled symptoms. However, a more comprehensive approach is often necessary to ensure that all of your mental, physical, and social needs are fulfilled.

Prevention

There is no effective way to avoid mental illness. If you have a mental illness, however, taking efforts to reduce stress, build resilience, and boost low self-esteem may help you keep your symptoms under control.

Self-Help for Women in Mental Health

Self-care practices and general lifestyle modifications can aid in the management of the symptoms of many mental health issues.

Pay Attention to Warning Signs

Consult with your doctor or therapist to determine what may be causing your problems. Make a strategy so you'll know what to do if your symptoms return. If you notice any changes in your symptoms or how you feel, contact your doctor or therapist. Consider taking the advice of family members or friends and keep an eye out for warning signs.

Keep A Mood Journal

Tracking your moods may assist you in determining what makes you feel better or worse. You can then take actions to prevent, modify, or prepare for mental challenges. You may make a mood diary or discover one online - as several phone applications are available for free on the internet.

Boost Your Self Esteem

Taking efforts to boost your self-esteem might help you feel more confident and productive. Be kind and love yourself by taking good care of your diet, and sleep. Recognize your self-worth.

Nourish Your Social Life

It is important to feel connected to other people. It can make you feel important and secure in yourself, and it can provide you with a unique perspective on things. Start attending community events where you might share common interests or experiences with other members, or joining a group such as a local literature club or sports team.

Try Peer Support

When you have a mental health problem, you can feel as if no one understands you. Peer support brings together people who have had similar experiences to support one another. This can have several advantages, including:

- Feeling accepted for who you are
- Boosts self-confidence
- Allows yourself to meet new people, and use your experiences to help others
- Discovering new information, ideas, and support for help in the face of stigma and discrimination

Make Time for Therapeutic Activities

You can safely practice a variety of methods and therapies on your own.

Relaxation

You may already be aware of what helps you relax, such as taking a bath, listening to music, or taking your dog for a walk. If you know that a certain hobby makes you feel calmer, make time for it.

Mindfulness

Mindfulness is a therapeutic method challenging you to become more aware of the present moment. This can apply to both the external environment and your inner feelings and ideas. Practicing mindfulness can help you become more aware of your emotional reactions.

Getting into Nature

Getting out into nature, such as a park or the countryside, is very beneficial. Even if you don't have a garden or are limited in your mobility, caring for plants or animals may help you get the advantages of nature.

Take Care Of Your Physical Health:

By maintaining physical health you can also manage your mental health.

Get Enough Sleep

When you can, take a long break. This can provide you the energy you need to deal with difficult feelings and emotions.

Physically Active

Regular exercise does not have to be difficult to be useful - to begin, try mild exercises such as going for a small walk, yoga, or swimming. The most important thing is to choose something you like doing so that you will be more likely to stay with it.

Avoid Drugs and Alcohol

While you may prefer to use drugs or alcohol to cope with unpleasant emotions, they might make you feel even worse in the long term.

Mind Your Personal Care

When you're struggling with a mental health issue, it's easy for personal care to fall away. But, simple actions like having a shower and getting dressed can have a significant impact on how you feel.

Eat Healthily

When and what you eat has a great impact on your mental health, too. Eating healthy leads to good mental health. Also, it helps you stay more positive and energetic.

Recognize You Need Professional Help

Ignoring until symptoms worsen can make it much more difficult to treat mental health issues. Long-term maintenance care can also assist to avoid relapses of symptoms. Visit regularly your psychotherapist for the betterment of mental health.

Develop Recovery Plan

If you are dealing with a mental health problem, you should develop a written recovery plan.

Recovery plans

- Allow you to set healthy objectives
- Describe what you can do to achieve those objectives
- Include both everyday activities and long-term goals
- Keep track of any changes in your mental health issues

Stigma and Myths Related to Mental Illness

Unfortunately, not everyone is aware of mental health problems. Some people may have misunderstandings regarding the meaning of certain diagnoses. They may also use dismissive, rude, or cruel words. This may be quite unpleasant, especially if the person experiencing these feelings from a family member, coworker, or healthcare professional.

Myths

Mental health problems are not associated with children.

People with mental health illnesses are aggressive and unpredictable.

People with mental health problems, even those who are managing their mental illness, are unable to deal with the stress of the job.

There is no hope for people diagnosed with mental illness. When a friend or family member develops mental health problems, he or she will never be able to recover.

Self-help and therapy are a waste of time. Why bother when a tablet will work fine?

I can't help someone who is dealing with a mental problem.

Prevention is useless. Mental disorders cannot be cured.

Takeaway

Our mental health is influenced by our emotional, psychological, and social well-being. It has an impact on the way we think, feel, and act. Your thinking, emotions, and behavior may be disrupted if you have mental health concerns at some point in your life. Neurotransmitters are natural substances in the brain that send signals to other regions of the body. People who suffer from mental illness are more likely to have a blood relative who suffers from the same ailment. Mental illnesses can be linked to environmental pressures, inflammatory diseases, toxins, alcohol, or narcotics while in the womb.

Mental illness is a primary cause of incapacity. Mental illness that goes untreated can lead to major emotional, behavioral, and physical health problems. The type of mental illness you have, the severity of the sickness, and what works best for you will all influence your treatment.

Contact your doctor or therapist if you notice any changes in your symptoms or how you feel. It is critical to experience a sense of belonging. It can make you feel significant and safe in yourself while also giving you a distinct viewpoint on things.

Start by visiting community events where you can meet new people and discuss mutual interests or experiences, or join an organization like a local literature club or sports team.

Chapter 3: Self-Help for Women in Depression and Anxiety

Depression, according to the American Psychiatric Association, is a medical condition that adversely affects the way you feel, think and act. The sad gloomy mental state makes you lose interest in your daily activities, and it has damaging effects on your mind, body, and soul.

Very often, depression doesn't have only a single cause. There can be multiple reasons when a person can have an episode of depression, with the severity being mild to alarming. Losing someone you loved, having a financial or economic crisis, failing in your personal life. Anything can trigger stress and a person can become depressed due to it.

Anxiety

Anxiety, on the other hand, is the bodily response to stressful episodes. The bouts of serious nervousness, tension, or worry can activate the anxiety attack. Depression and anxiety often reside along with each other, and they are somewhat a normal response to temporary life stressors, but if the episodes are recurrent and severe, then it can be an alarming situation and often requires professional help.

Depression and anxiety are a part of almost every individual's life, but studies show that depression occurs more in women than men. There are various reasons for it, starting with the hormonal influence. The ripe years of reproduction (25-45 years) pose more episodes of depression and anxiety due to the levels of estrogen and progesterone, which trigger the neurotransmitters in the brain that affects the mood swings in women. Also, the gender difference in society is itself a reason for women being more stressed than men. Social discrimination at the workplace, women having dual roles of being a housewife and a working person is a challenge. Above all, the family history of mood disorders and going through traumatizing events in early life also contribute to depression and anxiety.

Effects of Depression and Anxiety on Women

Depression and anxiety can impact different aspects of a woman's life. Physical health is compromised and women feel weak and destructed. Your body feels fatigued and lethargic. Also, the body's immunity is compromised and you tend to catch infections more frequently. Your heart function is also affected and there is a higher risk of heart attack and other cardiac anomalies. Your gut health is disturbed as well, and Irritable bowel Syndrome can occur as it is triggered by stress and anxiety. The social life of a woman is also affected due to depression and anxiety. A person feels isolated and does not want to face the people around him. Everyday activities are compromised, and a person feels lonely and doubts one's self-worth. Mental health is affected the most by depression and anxiety. This dire and strong grief, sadness, sense of guilt, and hopelessness are true and clear signs of depression. A person starts to have a pessimistic thought process and they tend to think negatively about every aspect of their lives.

How to Overcome Depression

These fleeting spells of depression can be addressed with the help of one's willpower and inner strength to cope with the stressful condition. There is nothing that can be done unless you are willing to do it. Depression is a common condition that is a part of almost every individual living, but the bodily response to it is different in every person, and the way to deal with it is also unique and individualized.

The first and foremost point is to get a grip on your life and accept the fact that depression is affecting your body and mind and that you need to fight it. Accepting is the first step to self-help.

Reach out for social support. Being with people who genuinely care for you is an essential step to be taken for the betterment of the condition. If you just stay in depression without seeking help or talking to someone, things might not get better and you cannot move towards a better healthier perspective of life. This is not easy, as a person tends to become socially isolated and does not interact positively in a social environment. Reaching out with the sole purpose of getting help can be a wise decision to beat the depression and feel better.

Prioritize your health. It is a great way to cope with episodes of depression. Setting a healthy sleep routine and aiming for 8 hours of sleep can help avoid sleeping problems related to depression and anxiety.

Self-care is a helpful technique to feel good about yourself. Looking after oneself, doing the things that you genuinely enjoy can be favorable in dealing with depression and anxiety.

Exercise and Depression

Physical exercise has proven to be an effective tool to energize the body and decrease the feeling of tiredness and fatigue. The ideal timing of 30 minutes is optimum to boost the body and feel thrilled. But yes, it is a challenging task to initiate the exercise routine and to keep up with it. Listen to your body and find the exercise routine that suits better to your body. If 30 minutes seems tiring, then a 10-minute exercise sprint 3 times a day is equally effective. Find the exercises your body enjoys doing, such as swimming, walking, dancing, yoga, sports, etc.

Diet and its Effect on Depression

Eating the right type of diet has a pivotal effect on the way your body and mind respond. For women dealing with depression and anxiety, a consultation with a registered dietician can help you a lot to keep your mind and body in a healthy state. Eating after every 3-4 hours is important as skipping meals makes you feel tired and weary. Keeping yourself hydrated is also important to cope with depression. Some vitamins have a beneficial effect on depression and anxiety. Nutrients like omega 3 fatty acids, Vitamin B6, Vitamin C, Vitamin E, Calcium, and Magnesium are scientifically proven to be positive elements in combating depression. Low levels of iron, B vitamins, and folic acid can trigger depression and anxiety. The last but most important point related to diet is avoiding refined sugars, alcohol, caffeine, high salt, and fatty fried food. This is a very important step to keep the body and mind off all the toxins and oxidative free radicals.

Avoiding alcohol and other illicit drugs is very important as it can worsen mental health functioning. They might temporarily alleviate the symptoms of depression, but they have damaging effects on your mind. Sidestepping on drugs and alcohol has proven to be helpful to combat depression and anxiety.

Studies have shown that sunlight is a useful tool to reduce depression and anxiety as it produces serotonin, a hormone that reduces stress and improves mood. Sitting for 10-15 minutes with sunscreen applied and not directly facing the sun can be beneficial.

Shun all the negative thoughts that come to your mind. The common symptom of depression is feeling hopeless and a pessimistic state of mind, and a person starts to think in the same negative way routinely. It is important to realize that these thoughts are merely distracting your mind. Therefore, try to keep your mind off such destructive thoughts.

Spending some time close to nature, going to the beach, going for a hike, getting your pet out for a walk, walking on wet grass are some ways that can nurture your soul and can help you find the sense and meaning of life. Going to the mosque, church, or your religious temples and talking to your spiritual counselors is favorable for spiritual well-being.

Spending time with the person you love is the best therapy to beat depression. Going for a drive, a cup of coffee, a long walk or simply chatting with your favorite person you trust and talk your heart out is the best meditation. It helps you feel better and positive.

Peer group therapies are also available for people with similar experiences to talk and support each other. This makes them feel like they are not the only ones going through depression. Numerous support groups in every part of the world can provide their kind help.

Writing about your feelings in a diary or journal can be helpful for healing, too. This can help you express your emotions and keep track of your thoughts.

This can be an outlet for the thoughts and feelings and a coping mechanism for depression and anxiety.

If all these self-help approaches are not helping, and a woman needs a lot more than self-help techniques to overcome depression, then you should seek help from mental health professionals. Numerous psychotherapies, talk therapies, and cognitive-behavioral therapies are very supportive in dealing with anxiety and depression. Moreover, anti-depressant medications can help relieve the symptoms of depression in women.

All of the self-help strategies mentioned above are dependent on the person's severity of depression and anxiety, and also on the interest and state to use the strategies to get out of this damaging state. Forcing someone to get into these supportive therapies is not useful. Instead, encourage the person to escape the toxic cycle of depression and anxiety and ask them to find the yearning within them to become a better version of themselves.

Takeaway

A person may experience an episode of depression for a variety of reasons, ranging from moderate to severe. Anxiety attacks can be triggered by episodes of severe anxiousness, stress, or worry. Depression and anxiety are frequently found together. They're a typical reaction to temporary life stressors, but if they're persistent and severe, it's a serious problem that generally necessitates expert assistance.

Depression and anxiety can affect a woman's life in a variety of ways. Women's physical health is being jeopardized, and they are feeling weak and destroyed. You're tired and sluggish.

These brief bouts of depression can be managed by using one's inner strength and resolve to cope with the stressful situation. Nothing is impossible if you are ready to put forth the effort. Things might not get better if you continue in depression without seeking help or talking to someone, and you won't be able to move toward a better, healthier outlook on life. It's also crucial to stay hydrated when dealing with depression. Some vitamins have antidepressant and anti-anxiety properties. It can be useful to sit for 10-15 minutes with sunscreen on and not directly facing the sun. Numerous support groups from all around the world are willing to lend a hand.

Chapter 4: Self-Help for Women in Divorce

Life is full of ups and downs. Sometimes, it is like a blooming flower, making everything beautiful by spreading its fragrance and color, but at times it shows its worst side, full of grieves and sorrows. We can never know which road life has chosen for us. It's easy to cherish all the love and affections life grants us, yet the real art is to face the ugly and strenuous aspect of life with audacity and fortitude. Divorce is one of the challenging phases as it changes your life altogether. It is a complicated process, both emotionally and legally. Many couples try to hold to their marriage and sort their affairs out, but in the end, they came to realize that divorce is the only option left. Divorce is a great loss; loss of a partner, loss of companionship, loss of dreams and commitment.

Divorce is an agonizing change, especially for women. It is a tumultuous time of stress, both financially and emotionally. If it's about husband and wife only, it's easy but it becomes harder if it involves children as their life is reflected by their parent's decision. There is a complete alteration of life during and after divorce. It is a painful patch of life that is not easy to overcome. Moreover, some women face such miseries in their marital life that divorce is the only and better option left and is a necessary decision. In such situations, divorce makes you feel light and lifts the burden off the shoulders. It may sound easy and uncomplicated, but it is a great battle that a woman has to fight alone, facing all the dilemmas of life and defending herself from the never-ending questions of people around her. But still, she has to move on in her life and for this, a woman has to work on herself. Self-help is the only and better option for a divorced woman. Practicing self-care will allow her to feel lighter and stress-free.

Here are some of the tips which can help to focus on self-help for women in divorce and can help them find a way:

Love yourself

Whatever the reason for the split is, no doubt your life will turn upside down in divorce. So, it is important to try to keep things as normal as possible. It is a hard pill to swallow but remember, nothing is impossible! Do not skip your meals in anxiety and depression and do not change your sleep patterns. Do the things you love to do the most, like reading books, watching movies, listening to some songs, etc. Experience new things that will make you hopeful about your future. Utilize your newfound time by enjoying doing things you have always wanted to do. All of this will help you to maintain a positive attitude. Keep yourself first and everything else next. Never doubt yourself. Consider yourself powerful enough to fight your battles alone. You are the strongest pillar to rely on, get through this hard time bravely.

Gaining emotional strength

Divorce is not an easy step to take. It needs a conscious decision and lots of courage. During the whole process of divorce, you have to strengthen up yourself. Women are always taught that they are born to give care and love, however, the reality is women deserve care and love equally. If you know your worth, this will help you to gain emotional independence instantly. The Coping mechanism is different for each person. Some require less time and effort to get over hard times. However, at the same time, only a few people bring themselves out of such a time quickly. But as for a divorce, there are different ways. First, stop asking yourself, "did I make the right choice for myself?" This question in your mind will never let you move forward. Whatever has happened is in the past, now start a new life with all the positive thoughts and energy. Secondly, you can get emotional independence and support with the help of someone. A professional therapist can be of great help in this regard. Your trustworthy close friends and family members could be a good option to help in rebuilding your self-esteem. The people around you can play a great role in emotional strengthening. Tell yourself that you have done nothing wrong but only what's best for you.

Amend your routine

Do not let your inner-self get lost in the phase of sorrow and misery. Don't make yourself feel guilty or a victim. If you want to make yourself more comfortable with the new phase of life try out new things, explore the place you are living in, or do what you love. It will surely help you to feel whole again. Altering your daily routine and changing your habits will help you to rediscover your inner peace. Married life has altogether a different routine, doing your daily chores until the clock runs out. You don't have enough time for yourself and follow the same pattern every day like a wind-up toy. Now it's time to change your routine and add on things which you have always wanted to do the whole time. Make yourself useful and enjoy every day. Little life changes can be very meaningful and essential. Keep yourself busy with the things you like, meet people with whom you feel better, or develop new hobbies which will keep your mind occupied.

Financial autonomy

Besides emotional strength, a woman needs to empower herself financially as well. Right after a divorce, you are asked a question, "what will be your source of income?" It may be challenging because to live independently, you need to work on your economic conditions. Usually women in a state of "limbo" work on their emotional issues, but for mental peace, it takes both emotional and economic stability. So, start to educate yourself on how to work on your financial conditions. This can be done by budgeting. To explain it more easily, take a look at your total monthly living income and expenses. If the net is positive and you have enough money to spare, then you are in a safe zone. But if the net is negative, then you are in a bit of trouble as it will make it difficult for you to live a stress-free life. Eventually, you will have to cut down on your expenses. In a nutshell, divorced women must look after their budget and maintain their financial position.

Do what you love

It is truly said that we give up parts of ourselves in a relationship. But now is the time to rediscover yourself again. Do what you love the most. This could be shopping, going on a trip, taking cooking classes, etc. You can learn something different and new. This can help you to overcome negative thoughts. Best of all, make yourself a bucket list. Write everything you have always wanted to do in your life and do them accordingly. This will bring change to you and will boost your confidence.

Get active

As we all have already heard, "a healthy body has a healthy mind." This perfectly fits into the situation of divorce. If you want to keep your mind off your past, you have to make efforts for it. Exercise is the best start for this. Physical exercise will relieve your body from stressful thoughts and will help you to revive your spirit. It will make you feel fresh and energetic. Work out or any other physical activity will be a great step forward to wrap up your frustration and make you feel like a whole new person again. Once you get into a pattern of work out it provides you inner peace and happiness. You feel great when you see desired results showing up in your physical appearance.

Revolutionize your environment

To feel different and fresh, you can change your aura. It can involve your house or your friend circle. Make little changes around yourself to feel more alive. For example, change your room settings or curtains, buy new furniture, plant some flowers, etc. Furthermore, make new friends who can help you to think positively and benefit you in growing. Environment makes a great impact on one's life. Even a simple house décor or growing plants can bring positivity to your life. Adding different colors to your surroundings can change your whole mood and can make you feel fresh.

Eat...but eat healthily

It's a fact that in stressful conditions, people ignore their health by skipping meals or eating too much, disturbing their sleep patterns, and neglecting physical exercise. Always remember physical health lays the foundation of your mental health as well as emotional wellbeing. Eat small frequent meals. Add fresh fruits and vegetables to your diet. Have some salads or fresh juices. Opposite to that, avoid stress-eating strictly. Say no to chocolates, donuts, cakes, and soft drinks.

Eat right! Invest your time in trying out new healthy food recipes. Invite your family or friends and cook for them.

Thus, we should all know that life is not a fairy tale. But always remember, whether we have chosen divorce or divorce has chosen us, you will survive. Making small efforts can bring drastic changes in a women's life. So don't give up!

Takeaway

Divorce is a difficult transition, especially for women. It's a chaotic period of financial and mental stress. It's simple if it's only between husband and wife, but it becomes more difficult when children are involved, as their lives are influenced by their parents' decisions. It may appear straightforward, but it is a major struggle that a woman must fight alone, facing all of life's challenges and defending herself against the never-ending questioning of those around her.

It's a difficult pill to take, but keep in mind that nothing is truly impossible!

If you're suffering from anxiety or depression, don't miss meals or modify your sleeping patterns. Do the things you enjoy most, such as reading books, watching movies, listening to music, and so on. You must maintain your strength throughout the divorce procedure. Women are taught that they are born to care for and love others, but the reality is that all women deserve to be cared for and loved equally. If you realize how much you're worth, you'll be able to help others acquire emotional independence almost immediately. In a nutshell, a divorced woman must maintain her financial situation by managing her budget.

Do what you really want to do. This could include things like going shopping, taking a trip, or taking cooking classes. To feel more alive, make small adjustments around you.

Change your room's decor or curtains, get new furniture, plant some flowers, and so on. It's a reality that in stressful circumstances, people neglect their health by skipping meals or eating excessively, disrupting sleep patterns, and avoiding physical activity. Eat healthily! Spend some time experimenting with new healthy meal recipes. You can cook for your family or friends if you invite them over.

Chapter 5: Self-Help in Health

What is Health?

This definition is approved by the Centers for Disease Control and Prevention, including a range of WHO partners.

"Complete physical, mental and social well-being and not merely the absence of disease or infirmity."

Also, defined by the other three possible definitions:

First definition

The absence of any disease or impairment is described as health.

Second definition

Health is a state in which an individual can cope with all of life's needs (implying also the absence of disease and impairment).

Third definition

Health is a state of balance, an equilibrium maintained by an individual within himself as well as between himself and his social and physical environment.

What Is Wellness?

Wellness is defined by the WHO as:

"the optimal state of health of individuals and groups"

Health Vs. Wellness

Health is a state of being that includes everything from physical health to social and emotional health. While holistic health is the target, health is usually achieved by evaluating the areas that require attention and taking actions to treat each of them.

Wellness

The act of practicing healthy habits daily to achieve better physical and mental health results is known as wellness. Essentially, health is the end goal, but wellness is the dynamic process of living a healthy and fulfilling life. Wellness refers to the different aspects of our lives that have an impact on our health and well-being.

Components of Health

The most important health takeaways are that it is important to maintain and focus on all **eight** dimensions of health.

The two most often mentioned types of health are probably **mental** and **physical** health. These have been linked by medical experts to lower stress levels and improved mental and physical well-being.

- mental
- physical

- social
- emotional
- spiritual
- environmental
- occupational
- intellectual, and physical wellbeing

By self-caring, we can play a vital role in maintaining and promoting healthy functioning and enhance well-being.

What is Self-Care?

Self-care is based on strategic actions taken to promote one's physical, mental, and emotional health. Self-care may have various forms and types. It can be as simple as getting enough sleep each night or going out for a few minutes to get some fresh air.

Self-care is essential for developing resilience to life's inevitable challenges. You'll be better equipped to live your best life if you've taken efforts to care for your mind and body.

However, unfortunately, many individuals consider self-care to be a luxury rather than a need. It is essential to consider how you care for yourself in a variety of domains to ensure that you are caring for your mind, body, and soul.

Basics of Self Care to Maintain Good Health

Committing to self-care is one of the most valuable gifts you can offer to yourself and others around you. You can act as a role model to your family, friends, and coworkers by taking care of your health.

Physical Self-Care

Balanced Diet and Healthy Choices

Make sure to fill half of your plate with fruits and vegetables. Fill up the rest of your meal with a variety of proteins and whole grains. Make it simple by understanding food serving sizes, health benefits, and guidelines for each food category.

Stay Hydrated

Water, clear non-caffeinated drinks, and meals are all considered to be part of your daily fluid intake. Avoid high-sugar sports drinks and sodas, or choose water-rich fruits and vegetables. Start your every day with a full glass of water and maintain the habit throughout the day, including at mealtimes. Men should take at least 8-12 ounces glasses of water per day, while women should aim for 8-9 ounces glasses of water per day. Drinking throughout the day rather than all at once allows your body cells to absorb the water gradually, reducing stress on your kidneys.

Limit Alcohol Intake

If you drink alcoholic beverages, the Dietary Guidelines for Americans recommend that you do so in moderation, with no more than one drink per day for women and two drinks per day for men. That is equivalent to 12 ounces of beer, 8 ounces of malt liquor, 5 ounces of wine, or 1.5 ounces of 80-proof distilled spirits or liquor (e.g., gin, rum, vodka, or whiskey). Excessive or binge drinking involves a series of immediate and long-term health risks.

Avoid Tobacco Usage

No list would be complete without mentioning the numerous reasons why smoking is harmful. If you are a smoker, this is going to be one of the toughest habits to change. Share cigarette cessation programs with your family and friends.

Go for a Walk

Walking opportunities are available, whether it's taking a 10-minute walk break at work or using the stairs instead of the elevator. These small movements can boost blood flow, releasing hormones that help us manage stress, increase alertness, and burn calories.

Stay Physically Active

Adults should aim for at least 30 minutes of moderate-intensity movement each day of the week, whether that is 30 minutes at a time or in 10-minute steps three times a day, as per experts. Find an activity that you enjoy and you will look forward to working out.

Maintain Hygiene

The most effective approach to prevent the transmission of germs is to properly wash your hands. It's the simplest action you can take to protect yourself and others from disease. Hand cleaning with soap and water is still the most efficient approach. When soap and water are not easily available, an alcohol-based hand sanitizer (containing at least 60% alcohol) is advised as a backup option.

Healthy Sleep Patterns

Adhering to a sleep schedule or bedtime practices, such as going to bed and waking up at the same time every day, can reinforce your body's "sleep-wake" cycle. Relaxing habits, such as reading a book or listening to music, help your body wind down at the end of the day.

Go for Regular Checkup

Your general physician will assist you in staying healthy, treating illness, and disease prevention. Request a list of general health screening recommendations from your doctor to assess the need for an appointment.

Set A Goal for Your Health

For optimum good health, you need to establish specific goals for your health with measurable results. These are the kinds of goals you're more likely to pursue as part of a long-term commitment to greater health and fitness.

Mental Self-Care

The way you think and the things you fill your mind with have a major effect on your psychological well-being.

Doing activities that keep your mind sharp, such as puzzles or learning about a subject that you are interested in, is an example of mental self-care. Reading books or viewing movies that inspire you may help to feed your brain.

Doing things that help you stay mentally well is also part of mental self-care. Self-compassion and acceptance, for example, can help you in maintaining a better inner dialogue.

For maintenance of mental self-care, you should ask yourself two questions:

1. Are you dedicating enough time to cognitively stimulating activities?

1. Are you taking proactive activities to maintain your mental health?

Social Self-Care

Self-care involves socializing. However, when life becomes busy, it's difficult to make time for friends, and it's easy to ignore your relationships.

Close relationships are essential for your well-being. The simplest method to develop and preserve close relationships is to invest time and effort in establishing relationships with people.

There is no need to spend a certain amount of time with your friends or working on your relationships daily. Everyone's social needs are slightly varied. The key is to determine your social demands and to provide sufficient time in your schedule to build an ideal social life.

You can assess your self-care practices by asking yourself the following two questions:

1. Do you spend enough time with your friends in person?

1. What are you doing to improve your bonds with friends and family?

Emotional Self-Care

It is essential to have healthy coping skills when dealing with unpleasant emotions such as anger, anxiety, and sadness. Activities that help you recognize and express your feelings regularly may be termed emotional self-care.

It's important to include emotional self-care into your life, whether you chat to a spouse or close friend about how you're feeling or set aside time for leisure activities that help you process your emotions.

You can assess your emotional health by emotional self-care questioning strategies. These questions are:

1. Do you have a healthy way of dealing with your emotions?

1. Do you include activities in your life that help you recharge?

Spiritual Self-Care

Nurturing your spirit does not have to include religion automatically. It can include everything that helps in the development of a greater feeling of meaning, understanding, or connection with the universe.

Spiritual self-care is essential whether you prefer meditating, attending religious services, or praying.

Spiritual health care progress can be assessed by two of the following questions:

1. What are some of the questions you have regarding your life and experiences?

1. Are you participating in spiritual activities that you find fulfilling?

Takeaway

Health is a condition of equilibrium, which an individual maintains both inside himself and between himself and his social and physical environment. We may play an important role in sustaining and fostering healthy functioning and enhancing well-being by taking care of ourselves.

Self-care entails taking proactive steps to improve one's physical, mental, and emotional well-being. Self-care can come in a variety of shapes and sizes. It might be as simple as getting adequate sleep each night or getting some fresh air for a few minutes.

Aim for at least 8-12 ounces glasses of water per day for men and 8-9 ounces glasses of water per day for women. Drinking beverages throughout the day rather than all at once allows your body cells to progressively absorb the water, reducing the risk of dehydration.

Your primary care physician can help you stay healthy, manage illnesses, and prevent disease. To determine the need for a visit, ask your doctor for a list of general health screening recommendations.

Whether you talk to a spouse or close friend about how you're feeling or set aside time for leisure activities that help you process your feelings, it's critical to integrate emotional self-care into your life.

Everything that aids in the development of a higher sense of meaning, understanding, or connection with the cosmos can be included.

Chapter 6: Self-Help in Trauma

What Is Trauma?

Trauma is defined as an individual's response to a severely disturbing or distressing experience (natural disaster, accident, rape, etc.) that overwhelms their ability to cope, induces feelings of helplessness, and limits their sense of self-esteem and ability to feel a full range of emotions and experiences.

Not everyone who goes through a traumatic situation develops trauma. There are also several types of trauma. Some people can experience symptoms that will go away within a few weeks, while others will suffer long-term symptoms.

A traumatized person can experience a variety of feelings. They may feel overwhelmed, hopeless, or stunned, or they may fail to process their experiences. Physical symptoms can also be caused by trauma.

With treatment, people can address the underlying causes of their trauma and find constructive methods to manage their symptoms.

Types of Trauma

There are several types of traumas:

Acute Trauma: is caused by a single stressful or risky incident.

Chronic Trauma: is associated with prolonged and persistent exposure to very stressful conditions. Cases of child abuse, bullying, or domestic violence are examples.

Complex Trauma: occurs as a result of multiple traumatic events.

Vicarious Trauma: is another type of trauma known as secondary trauma. As for this type of trauma, a person is getting trauma symptoms as a result of direct contact with someone who has been through a traumatic event.

Sometimes secondary or vicarious trauma symptoms persist and their severity increases with time, more likely a person might develop a mental health problem known as Post Traumatic Stress Disorder.

Factors of Trauma

A traumatic event can impact a person in a variety of ways, including:

- the occurrence of other mental health problems
- before traumatic event exposure
- the form and characteristics of the event or events
- their experience and ability to regulating emotions

Symptoms

There are several symptoms after facing trauma, some are emotional, psychological, and physical symptoms.

- denial
- anger
- fear
- sadness
- shame
- confusion
- anxiety
- depression
- numbness
- guilt
- hopelessness
- irritability
- difficulty concentrating

- denial
- anger

Treatment

Several treatments can assist people who have experienced trauma in dealing with their symptoms and improving their quality of life.

- Therapy
- Cognitive-behavioral therapy
- Eye movement desensitization and reprocessing
- Somatic and other therapies
- Medication

Self-Care in Trauma

Self-care can help people cope with the emotional, psychological, and physical effects of trauma. Self-care for trauma includes the following examples: Everyone's concept of self is different. It is essential to pay attention to your body and what it needs. Our bodies are often very tuned in to what we require and will let us know so that we may begin to heal. While there is no specific solution to healing trauma, there are a few things you may try!

Don't Isolate Yourself

You may want to isolate yourself after a traumatic event, but this just makes matters worse. Face-to-face contact with others will contribute to your healing, so maintain your relationships and avoid spending too much time alone.

Don't Talk About Your Trauma

Connecting with people does not have to involve sharing the trauma. In fact, for some people, this can make the situation worse. Feeling engaged and valued by others brings comfort.

Seek Support

You must have someone with whom you can share your feelings face to face, someone who will listen carefully without judging you. Take the advice of a trusted family member, friend, counselor, or preacher.

Take Part in Social Activities and Try to Reconnect with Your Old Friends

Even if you don't want to, do "normal" tasks with other people that have nothing to do with the traumatic event. Try to participate in social activities, gatherings, and events. Plan a reunion with your old friends to spend quality time.

Support Group for Trauma Survivors

Connecting with people who are dealing with similar issues can make you feel less isolated, and hearing how others cope can motivate you in your recovery.

Volunteer

Volunteering can be a good strategy to overcome the sense of helplessness that often comes with trauma. Helping others can help you remind yourself of your strengths and restore your sense of power.

Making New Friends

If you live alone or are apart from family and friends, it is important to go out and make new friendships. Take a class or join a club to meet people who share the same interests, join an alumni club, or reach out to friends or colleagues.

Get Back to Your Routine

A traumatic event can interrupt one's regular life. One aim for people trying to recover from trauma is to return to a normal lifestyle as soon as possible. Getting back into your groove can help you reestablish a sense of normalcy and recover control over your life.

Identify the Triggered Actions

In addition to promoting self-care after trauma, it can be beneficial to identify any triggers related to your traumatic event. You are more likely to enhance your sense of safety if you identify these triggers. Identifying places and people who make you feel comfortable can be helpful, as avoiding areas that make you feel uncomfortable.

Self-Regulate Your Nervous System

No matter how frustrated, disturbed, or out of control you feel, it's important to know that you can change your nervous system and calm yourself. It will not only assist to reduce the anxiety associated with trauma, but it will also give a better sense of control.

Stay Grounded

Sit on a chair to feel more present and grounded. Feel the ground near your feet and your back against the chair. Look around yourself and pick six objects that include red or blue. Catch your breath so you become more relaxed.

Mindful Breathing

If you're feeling confused or agitated, practicing mindful breathing can help you calm down quickly. Simply take 60 deep breaths, concentrating your attention on each 'out' breath.

Sensory Input

Is there a specific sight, smell, or flavor that immediately makes you feel calm? Sometimes petting an animal or listening to music will immediately calm you down. Everyone responds differently to sensory input, so try out different fast stress relief methods to see what works best for you.

Celebrate life

Even after a traumatic event, it is important to understand that it is OK to experience joy, celebrate successes, and enjoy the love of family and friends. It's all part of the process of healing.

Take good care of your health and become physically active!

Having a healthy mind and body can increase the ability to deal with stress and trauma.

Get Plenty of Sleep

Tension or fear may disturb your sleep patterns after a traumatic experience. However, a lack of quality sleep can worsen your trauma symptoms and make it harder to maintain your emotional balance. Sleep and wake up at the same time each day, and aim for 7 to 9 hours of sleep each night.

Balanced Diet

Eating small, well-balanced meals throughout the day will help you maintain your energy and reduce mood swings. To improve your mood, avoid sugary and fried foods and consume plenty of omega-3 fats, such as salmon, walnuts, soybeans, and flaxseeds.

Avoid Alcohol and Drugs

Their use can increase your trauma symptoms and increase feelings of depression, anxiety, and isolation.

Reduce Stress

Meditation, yoga, or deep breathing exercises are all simple ways to relax. Make time for activities that make you happy.

Physical Active

If it is more feasible, three 10-minute bursts of exercise each day are just as effective. Walking, jogging, swimming, basketball or even dancing works best since it uses both your arms and legs.

When to Seek Professional Help

It takes time to recover from trauma, and everyone heals at their own pace. However, if months have passed and your symptoms have not healed, you may require professional help from a trauma therapist.

Seek help when...

- Having trouble functioning at home or work
- Suffering from severe fear, anxiety, or depression
- Unable to form close, satisfying relationships
- Experiencing terrifying memories, nightmares, or flashbacks
- Emotionally numb and disconnected from others
- Using alcohol or drugs to feel better

Understanding with Therapist

The quality of your relationship with your therapist is just as important. Choose a trauma specialist with whom you feel comfortable. Find another therapist if you do not feel safe and secure, respected, or understood.

<u>Ask yourself the following questions:</u>

Did you feel at ease discussing your issues with the therapist?

Did you believe the therapist understood what you were talking about?

Were your concerns taken seriously, or were they dismissed or lowered?

Were you treated with compassion and respect?

Do you believe you could trust the therapist?

Takeaway

Not everyone who is exposed to a distressing experience suffers from trauma. There are several sorts of trauma as well. Some people will have symptoms that will go away in a few weeks, while others will have symptoms that will last a long time.

A traumatized individual might feel a wide range of emotions, both in the immediate aftermath of the event and in the long run. When secondary or vicarious trauma symptoms linger and become more severe over time, a person is more likely to develop a mental health condition known as Post Traumatic Stress Disorder.

After a distressing occurrence, you may want to isolate yourself, but this would just make things worse. It is not necessary to share your trauma to connect with others.

Indeed, for some people, this may aggravate the condition. It is much better to feel engaged and valued by others.

Plan a get-together with old pals to spend quality time together. Throughout the day, eating small, well-balanced meals will help you retain your energy and reduce mood fluctuations.

Chapter 7: Self-Help For Dependents

What is dependence?

Dependence is defined as the inability to quit using a substance or engaging in an activity ignoring the fact that it is causing psychological and physical harm.

The term "dependence" doesn't always refer to a dependence on drugs like heroin or cocaine. Some dependences are also characterized by the inability to resist participating in activities such as gambling, eating, or working.

Dependence is defined by The American Society of Medicine as:

"a treatable, chronic medical disease involving complex interactions among brain circuits, genetics, the environment, and an individual's life experiences. People with dependence use substances or engage in behaviors that become compulsive and often continue despite harmful consequences."

Term Dependent Means:

a person who has an intense, chronic, physiological, or psychological need for habit-forming substances, behavior, or action.

Types of Dependence:

Apart from alcohol, the most common and serious type of dependence is drugs

- Cocaine
- Narcotics(opioids)
- Marijuana
- Heroine
- Nicotine

Causes of Dependence

Hooking drugs and behaviors can provide a pleasant "high" that is both physical and psychological. To achieve the same high, you will typically use more particular drugs or participate in behaviors for a longer period. Dependence gets increasingly harder to overcome over time.

Brain

Some people may try a substance or habit once and never return to it, whereas others become dependent on it. This is due in part to the frontal lobes of the brain. The frontal lobe allows people to prolong feelings of pleasure or satisfaction. The frontal lobe malfunctions in dependence, and reward is instant.

Chemical imbalances in the brain and mental problems like schizophrenia or bipolar disorder are other probable reasons for dependence. These abnormalities can lead to coping strategies that grow into dependences.

Early Exposure

The environment and culture also influence how a person responds to a substance or behavior. A person's social support system may be lacking or disrupted, which can lead to drug or behavioral dependence. Dependence can develop as a result of traumatic experiences that impair coping skills.

Symptoms

Following are the primary symptoms of dependence:

- Irregularities and decline grades in school
- Bad performance at work
- Become more sensitive towards anxiety, stress, and depression
- Relationship difficulties, which sometimes include lashing out against those who recognize the dependence
- An inability to quit taking the substance even though it is affecting health or personal problems, such as problems with jobs or relationships.
- A visible lack of energy in everyday activities
- Significant changes in appearance, including weight loss and a significant abandonment of hygiene
- Becoming defensive when interrogated about substance use

Stages of Dependence

The reactions of your brain and body in the early stages of dependence differ from those in the later stages.

The four stages of dependence are as follows:

1. Experimentation: Using or engaged in something out of curiosity
2. Regular or social: use or participate in social settings or for social reasons
3. Problem or risk: performs or engages in irrational behavior with no concern for the consequences
4. Dependence is defined as the usage or involvement in an activity on daily or multiple times per day basis, despite the apparent possibility of adverse consequences.

Complications of Dependence:

Untreated long-term dependence has its consequences

- Physical: like cardiovascular diseases, HIV/AIDS, liver, and neurological problems
- Psychological: emotional, anxiety, depression, anger
- Social: damaged relationship and hate
- Economic: debts and lead to bankruptcy

Treatment

Dependences of all kinds can be treated. Because dependence typically impacts many aspects of life, the best plans are comprehensive. Treatments will be aimed to assist you or anyone you know to stop seeking and indulging in their dependence.

Among the most common treatments are:

- Treatment based on medication (mental disorders)
- Behavioral and psychotherapies and counseling
- Self-help and support groups for ongoing treatments
- Inpatients treatment or medical services to treatment withdrawal
- Follow-up care at regular intervals to keep in check the effectiveness of treatment

Self-Help for Dependents

The most difficult step toward recovery for many people suffering from dependence is the very first one: admitting that you have a problem and trying to make a change. In dependence treatment, self-help is an action, not just a concept. The self-help treatment plan will assist you in implementing self-care practices into your everyday routine. Dependence recovery is more than sobriety.

Start Thinking About Change

Keep note of your drug use, including when and how much you use. This will give you a better view of the role the dependence is playing in your life.

List the advantages and risks of quitting, as well as the costs and advantages of continuing to take drugs.

How do drugs affect your social life? Think about the things which are important to you such as your partner, kids, friends, and parents.

Connect with People Who Are in Their Recovery Phase

Dependence, depression, anxiety, and other mental issues develop in isolation. To avoid relapse and combat signs of poor mental health, it is helpful to understand individuals and groups that will support you in your recovery and give you the abilities you need to stay sober.

Build Sober Social Circle

If your past social life was based on drugs, you may need to develop some new friends. It is important to surround yourself with sober people who will support your recovery. Consider taking a class, joining a church or civic group, volunteering, or attending community events.

Try Healthy Ways to Cope with Your Stress

There are healthier ways to keep your stress level in check. You can learn to manage your problems without falling back on your dependence. When you're confident in your ability to quickly de-stress, facing strong feelings isn't as intimidating or overwhelming.

Keep drugs craving and triggers in check!

Stay Away from Dependent Friends

Do not connect with friends who are still using drugs. Surround yourself with individuals who support your sobriety rather than those who encourage you to revert to old, destructive habits.

Avoid Clubs and Bars

Even if you don't have an alcohol problem, drinking decreases inhibitions and impairs judgment, which can easily lead to a relapse. Drugs are usually easily available, and the temptation to use them can be intense. Avoid going to places that you associate with drug abuse.

Be Upfront of Your History

If you need medical or dental treatment, be forthright and seek out a doctor that will work with you to either prescribe alternatives or the absolute least medicine required. You should never feel ashamed or humiliated about prior drug use, nor should you be denied painkillers. If this happens, find another provider.

Participate in Distracting Activity

Read, visit friends, watch a movie, get involved in a hobby, go on a hike or exercise. When you get involved in anything else, the cravings will subside.

Change Your Thoughts

When having a craving, many people tend to remember only the pleasant benefits of the drug and ignore the negative consequences. As a result, you may find it useful to remind yourself that using drugs will not make you feel better and that it might lead to financial disaster. It might be useful to keep these consequences on a small card with you at all times.

Look after your health

Regular exercise, adequate sleep, and healthy eating habits can help you keep your energy levels while reducing your stress levels. The more you can keep your health and well-being, the better it will be to stay sober.

Meditation

Go for a walk, have a picnic at the seashore, enjoy a regular visit to the park. Do yoga or meditate in nature.

Healthy lifestyle

A well-balanced diet improves your focus and energy levels. This also contributes to a steadier mood! Eating nutritional meals makes you feel good, and good health makes you less likely to be tempted by drugs or alcohol.

Exercise

Exercise offers a series of advantages when it comes to dependence rehabilitation. Exercise regularly can help to manage stress levels. Because of the dopamine release that happens when you exercise, it also functions as a mood enhancer.

Reduce Stress

Many people will experience relapse as a result of stress. Practicing self-care during dependence recovery reduces stress. Adequate sleep, exercise, and improving outcomes are all excellent stress-reduction methods.

Go for Treatment

Convince yourself that you need a doctor to make you feel better and help you in your journey of recovery from dependence. Explore treatment programs, and choose accordingly which you find best for your help.

Stick to your recovery plan, manage your drugs trigger and detoxify them.

Go for your behavioral counseling sessions, either alone or group sessions, identify the root cause and learn healthier coping skills.

Use your medication regularly as prescribed by doctors and also visit your doctor for follow-up check-ups.

Takeaway

Dependence is described as a person's inability to stop taking a substance or engaging in a behavior despite the knowledge that it causes psychological and bodily harm. Drugs and behaviors that are hooking can produce a pleasurable "high" that is both physical and psychological. You will often use more specific medications or engage in actions over a longer amount of time to attain the same high. Dependence becomes more difficult to overcome over time.

Other possible causes of dependence include chemical abnormalities in the brain and mental illnesses like schizophrenia or bipolar disorder. Dependence is a condition that develops over time.

The brain and body behave differently in the early stages of dependence than in the later stages.

It is beneficial to understand individuals and groups that will support you in your recovery and offer you the abilities you need to stay clean to avoid relapse and combat indicators of poor mental health. Take a walk, have a picnic along the beach, or pay a regular visit to the park. Practice yoga or meditate outdoors. Manage your drug triggers and detoxify them as part of your recovery approach.

Go to your individual or group behavioral counseling sessions to address the main problem and establish healthy coping techniques.

Chapter 8: Self-Help in Career for Women

Self-improvement is the process of improving one's abilities, skills, thinking, and so on through one's efforts. To put it another way, self-improvement is a result of your personal choice and work.

Commitment to self-improvement, combined with perseverance and attention, is a definite path to professional success. However, job success should not be defined solely in terms of advancement.

If this is your only goal, you may not be able to attain your goals. Your career will grow steadily if you improve your knowledge, experience, abilities, and efficiency on a broad scale. Self-improvement can be accomplished in a variety of ways:

Step Out of Your Comfort Zone

Getting out of your comfort zone is a crucial step toward self-improvement.

'A comfort zone is a wonderful location, but nothing grows there,' says a renowned quote. If you're content with your present knowledge and skills, you're either not growing or not willing to grow. You must be enthusiastic about learning more. Make an effort to improve yourself.

Seek Comprehensive Improvement

Self-improvement should not be restricted to a single aspect of your life. Make a plan to improve in all areas of your life. Continue to learn and re-learn. Make every effort to strengthen your skillset while simultaneously learning new ones. Consider each new day as an opportunity to improve yourself. Finally, all of your efforts will pay off not only in your personal life but also in your professional life.

Self-Reflection

Decide to examine your life objectively. It's pointless to lie to oneself, therefore be honest with yourself. Take note of areas in your life where you need to improve, whether professionally or personally, as you examine your life. Commit yourself to improve in those areas.

Be Responsible for Your Self-Improvement

Take on the task of continuously and progressively developing oneself. Make yourself accountable for your progress. Finally, the advantages of self-improvement will be enjoyed first by you before spreading to others. Make a list of areas where you want to improve and cross them off as you go. Career advancement is defined by your ambition and dedication to self-improvement, not by your status, qualifications, or background.

Continue to Act Foolishly

Learning is a never-ending process. Never assume you know everything about anything in your life or job. There's always something new to discover. It is easier to stay fascinated about life if you are eager to learn.

'Stay Hungry, Stay Foolish,' as Steve Jobs put it. Assimilate as much information as possible, develop your skillset, and enroll in pieces of training that will advance your profession.

You will remain stagnant not only in your profession but also in your life if you do not better yourself.

Continuous career progress occurs when you consistently increase your knowledge, abilities, experience, and efficiency. This means that if your primary goal is to advance in your career, you will almost certainly fail. However, if you are determined and persistent in your pursuit of self-improvement, the reward should be job success. With that in mind, here are some self-improvement tips that should help you advance in your profession.

Mistakes You May Make in Your Career

Making mistakes is a normal part of life. It can even be beneficial because it allows you to learn and develop. However, if you do not correct any errors, they will seriously impede your career advancement.

Various factors can jeopardize the future of decent, hardworking citizens. Honest errors frequently have severe effects. Here are the seven worst career mistakes that you can make.

1. Over Sharing

Boundaries must be respected at work. The dangers of disclosing too many personal details outweigh the benefits.

This isn't to say that we shouldn't make friends at work or let fear rule our lives. It simply means that we must use common sense in our professional interactions.

An employee who shows disappointment with their employer or informs co-workers that they are searching for a new position is asking for trouble.

1. Not Taking Responsibility

People avoid taking responsibility for a variety of reasons including laziness, fear of failure, and being overwhelmed by the scope of a problem.

Whatever the cause may be: if people refuse to accept responsibility, they will fail in their careers, their teams, and their personal growth. All of this emphasizes the importance of addressing the issue.

1. Asking About Perks Too Early

When you ask for a promotion or raise during an interview, you're telling the manager that you're more interested in what the organization can do for you than what you can do for it.

Employers understand that you want to advance your career, but don't look for another position until the one you want has been offered.

1. Lack of a Go Get Them Attitude

The people who lack a go-get-them attitude don't succeed in their careers. They get stuck at one point. People who have a "go get them attitude" have the following traits.

- They have dreams and aspirations
- They show up every day
- They count their victories
- They have what they love
- They have support

1. Getting Caught Up in Office Gossip

Workplace gossip can be extremely dangerous if the gossiper has considerable control over the recipient.

An emerging way of office gossip is via email. Since messages may easily be forwarded to unintended recipients, corporate e-mail can be an especially dangerous form of transmitting gossip.

The following are some of the negative effects of office gossip:

- It destroys trust and confidence
- Time and money are wasted
- Employees become more anxious as rumors spread without concrete details about what is and isn't true
- Employees become more polarized as they take sides
- Feelings and reputations are harmed
- Hardworking employees leave the office due to a toxic work environment

1. Not Creating a Budget

Lack of savings, financial instability, out-of-control spending, a higher risk of falling into debt, and increased financial stress are some of the most common effects of lack of budgeting.

Budgeting helps you to decide how you will invest your money and guarantees that you will still have enough money for the things you need and value.

Following a budget or spending plan will also help you stay out of debt or get out of debt if you're still in it.

Make financial arrangements to ensure that you can fulfill your needs both now and in the future. It is important to have a budget to fulfill your needs.

1. Following Someone Else's Career Path

Following someone else's career path by just looking at how successful they are is a huge mistake. Follow your dreams and career goals. Work hard to fulfill your dream rather than fantasizing about the quick money the other person is earning.

Little things can add up over time to destroy your career just as much as one major blunder. The good news is that if you remain aware of them, you can take control of them before they take over and destroy your career.

Personal Development Skills for Career Growth

Communication

Your ability to communicate includes your ability to speak, write, and listen. You can understand what people are saying and experiencing, as well as communicate your thoughts and feelings if you have these talents. Good communicators can talk clearly and confidently, with a positive and situation-appropriate tone.

Interpersonal

Interpersonal skills, often known as people skills or social skills, are the verbal and nonverbal behaviors and reactions to interactions with others. They have an impact on your ability to form social relationships and create an impression on others.

Organization

The neatness of your physical and digital areas, as well as your ability to plan, schedule, and prioritize, are all examples of organizational abilities. Good organization can help you save time, avoid misunderstandings, and increase efficiency.

Problem-Solving

Problem-solving skills refer to your ability to deal with difficult or unexpected situations. When confronted with a challenge, good problem-solvers maintain their composure and weigh all of their choices before deciding on the best course of action.

Self-Confidence

Confidence in one's abilities, actions, and decisions is referred to as self-confidence. If you believe in yourself, you are more inclined to set lofty goals, attempt new things, and believe in your ability to succeed.

Adaptability

Adaptability refers to your ability to rapidly and readily adjust to new situations. People who are good at dealing with change are more likely to get along with a wide range of personalities and prosper in a variety of situations. They may also maintain their composure in unexpected situations.

Integrity

People are more likely to trust those who are truthful and uphold their ideals. Integrity entails doing the right thing and stating the truth, even if it is difficult. Integrity can lead to a positive reputation and career chances.

Work Ethic

Work ethic encompasses not only hard work, but also dependability, accountability, quality, resolve, and discipline. People who have a strong work ethic are more productive and have a positive outlook.

Leadership is defined as the ability to lead others. Good leaders may inspire people and assist them in achieving a common objective. They boost morale and boost confidence.

How to Improve Your Personal Development Skills

Taking lessons, learning from others, developing new talents, and improving on current ones are all ways to improve your personal development skills. To help you grow as a person, follow these guidelines:

Face your fears and overcome them. You can't grow and progress if you're afraid.

Take a lesson or join a club that helps people become better public speakers if you're terrified of public speaking, for example. Find a mentor who can help you make excellent judgments and develop your confidence if you're afraid of taking risks. By trying out new things you may not be comfortable with, you will grow and learn.

If you're shy, try striking up a conversation or making an introduction to new individuals during a reunion.

Read

Reading can help you learn new things, expand your vocabulary, and stay informed. It can also boost your critical thinking skills by stimulating your mind. Set a goal for yourself to read at least one instructive or motivating article every day or one book per month.

Learn something new

Learn a new skill or subject, whether on your own or through a class. Take classes to learn a new language, a new software tool, or how to write creatively, for example. Consider attending a webinar about entrepreneurship or social media marketing for professional development.

Ask for feedback

Ask a family member, friend, or colleague for feedback on a recent effort or accomplishment.

Use both their favorable and constructive feedback to help you identify ways to improve. To acquire a new viewpoint, you sometimes need an outside, unbiased opinion.

Observe others

People who inspire you should be observed and learned from. Someone you know, such as a boss, a family member, or a public personality, could be the target.

Make a list of the qualities you appreciate about them and try to emulate them in yourself.

Network

You can discover new ideas and grasp how to communicate and cooperate with different personality types by interacting with a variety of people. You can also meet people and form ties with them that may prove beneficial in the future. Attend conferences and events on issues that interest you, or network through industry associations and shared interest groups.

Keep a journal

Every day or week, write in a notebook to improve self-awareness and reflect on previous experiences, decisions, and discussions. You can keep a handwritten, private notebook or blog about your thoughts and experiences. It can be used to set and track goals and progress.

Meditate

Meditation is used by many people to gain clarity and awareness, as well as to alleviate tension and worry. Meditation can assist you in focusing on your personal growth and goals in a healthy, positive, and tranquil manner. Even taking a break from work or scheduling some alone time might help you relax and focus.

Get a mentor

Speak with a mentor if you need assistance discovering methods to improve your self-development abilities. This person could be a boss, professor, someone you look up to, or a professional personal development mentor.

Personal Development Skills in The Workplace

While personal development skills can benefit you in all aspects of your life, the following habits may be particularly beneficial in the job and can help you enhance your career:

Be an active listener. Paying attention to what other people say is an important part of becoming a successful communicator. Focus on comprehending what your co-workers and clients are saying so you can remember it and answer appropriately. From phone conversations to job interviews, use effective and professional listening and communication skills.

Work well with others. You will be a valued team member if you have good people skills. You should be able to motivate and collaborate with others. Build relationships with co-workers, clients, customers, and acquaintances of various types and backgrounds by honing your social skills.

Organize your time, work, and materials. Plan out your duties so that you can get them done fast and easily. If you're working on multiple projects, know which ones to prioritize. You may be better able to meet deadlines and collaborate effectively with others if you are well-organized.

Work through challenging situations. Assess your alternatives and choose the best approach when dealing with an issue. Know when to seek counsel or conduct study into various scenarios. People who can think critically and solve complicated problems are more likely to make smart decisions in both their personal and professional lives.

Believe in yourself. Others are more inclined to believe in you if you are confident in your decisions. This pleasant energy has the potential to excite and inspire those around you. If you face obstacles with confidence rather than doubt, you will be better able to handle them and achieve your goals.

Adapt to change. Be adaptable so you can easily deal with changes at work and in your personal life. Adaptable people can operate well alone and in groups, manage several tasks, work in a range of environments, and accept new ideas, among other things. Being able to adapt to change effectively can make these situations less stressful for all parties involved.

Be truthful. The foundation of a strong relationship with co-workers and bosses is honesty. Maintain a high standard of ethics and adhere to your principles. Respect, satisfaction, and a good reputation at work can all be gained via integrity.

Be committed to and passionate about your job. People with a strong work ethic are more productive, dependable, and committed to producing high-quality results. This commitment might assist you in completing projects on schedule and motivating your coworkers.

Guide those around you. Being an effective leader involves self-assurance, foresight, and communication. People who have these leadership skills can assist their team in progressing and becoming more productive without becoming bossy.

Takeaway

Commitment to self-improvement, combined with perseverance and attention, is a definite path to professional success. However, job success should not be defined solely in terms of advancement.

You must be enthusiastic about learning more. Make an effort to improve yourself. Self-improvement should not be restricted to a single aspect of your life. Make a plan to improve in all areas of your life. Continue to learn and re-learn.

Decide to examine your life objectively. It's pointless to lie to oneself, therefore be honest with yourself. Take on the task of continuously and progressively developing yourself. Make yourself accountable for your progress. Finally, the advantages of self-improvement will be enjoyed first by you before spreading to others.

Learning is a never-ending process. Never assume you know everything about anything in your life or job. There's always something new to discover. Continuous career progress occurs when you consistently increase your knowledge, abilities, experience, and efficiency.

Take a lesson or join a club that helps people become better public speakers if you're terrified of public speaking, for example. Find a mentor who can help you make excellent judgments and develop your confidence if you're afraid of taking risks. Learn a new skill or subject, whether on your own or through a class. People who inspire you should be observed and learned from. Someone you know, such as a boss, a family member, or a public personality, could be the target. Make a list of the qualities you appreciate about them and try to emulate them in yourself.

Chapter 9: Self-Help for Happiness for Women

Social scientists have studied what makes us happy and what annoys us. We know that happiness predicts health and lifespan and that happiness measures may be used to assess societal development and policy effectiveness. Happiness, on the other hand, isn't something that just happens to you. Everyone can make modest adjustments in their behavior, environment, and relationships that can lead to a better life.

Every person has a propensity to be more like Eeyore than Tigger, dwelling on negative events rather than happy ones. Learning from hazardous or unpleasant circumstances we meet in life (bullying, trauma, betrayal) helps us avoid them in the future and respond swiftly in a crisis.

However, this means you'll have to put in a bit more effort to educate your brain to overcome negative ideas. Here's how to do it:

Don't try to stop yourself from having bad ideas!

"I have to stop thinking about this," you might tell yourself but this just makes you think about it more. Instead, take responsibility for your concerns. Recognize when you're stuck in a bad loop. "I'm concerned about my financial situation." "I can't stop thinking about job problems."

Treat yourself as though you were a friend!

When you're feeling bad about yourself, think about what advice you'd offer a buddy who was feeling low. Now try to put that advice into practice in your life.

Negative thoughts should be challenged!

The practice of confronting and correcting illogical beliefs is known as Socratic questioning. This approach has been shown in studies to help with depressive symptoms. The objective is to shift your mentality from one of failure ("I'm a failure.") to one of success ("I've had a lot of success in my career."). This is simply one setback that has nothing to do with me. I can improve as a result of it. Here are some questions to ask yourself to help you fight negative thinking.

To begin, write down your negative thoughts, such as "I'm experiencing difficulties at work and am doubting my skills."

Then ask yourself, "What proof do I have for this belief?"

"Am I speaking from experience? Or are these only feelings?"

"Could I be misreading the situation?"

"How do you think other individuals may see the situation?

"How would I react if this were to happen to someone else?"

The bottom line: We all have negative thoughts, but recognizing them and challenging them is a huge step toward living a better life.

Positive psychology experts have discovered that you may truly improve your happiness and general contentment with life and it doesn't involve a winning lottery ticket or any other significant shift in circumstances. It requires an inward shift in viewpoint and attitude. That's fantastic news since it's something that everyone can accomplish.

Myths about Happiness

There are many misconceptions regarding what would make you happy. So, before we get started on the methods that do work for increasing happiness, let's get rid of the ones that don't.

First Myth: Having a lot of money will make you happy

Being concerned about money is stressful. You do need enough of it to fulfill your fundamental requirements, such as food, housing, and clothes to be happy. However, once you have enough money to live comfortably, extra money won't make a significant difference in your happiness. Studies of lottery winners, for example, reveal that they are no happier after a very short amount of time than they were before their victory.

Second Myth: To be happy, you need to be in a relationship

While being in a good, supportive love relationship helps, it's not true that you can't be happy and content if you're single. Singles with significant connections and hobbies are, in fact, happier than those in unsuitable love relationships. It's also worth noting that even a happy marriage or love relationship doesn't guarantee long-term happiness. Expecting your spouse to fulfill your happy-ever-after wishes may cause long-term harm to your relationship. You are solely responsible for your happiness, not your spouse or family members.

Third Myth: As we become older, we become less happy

Contrary to conventional opinion, individuals grow happier as they get older. Seniors have more good feelings and fewer (and less severe) negative emotions than young individuals and middle-aged adults, according to a research study. In general, older individuals are happier with their life, are less stressed, and are more emotionally stable. For many people, it is the happiest time of their lives despite the losses that come with age.

Fourth Myth: Some individuals are simply happier than others, and you can do nothing about it!

Happiness is influenced by genetics. According to a recent study, humans are born with a happy "set point." However, this only accounts for roughly half of our overall satisfaction. Another 10% is related to personal situations. That leaves 40% of your life to be decided by your decisions and behaviors. That's a lot of authority!

Tips for finding joy in your life

Here are some suggestions to help you feel better:

Play some of your favorite tunes. It can help you recollect happy experiences, giving you a break from the problems you're dealing with daily. Listen to music while working, cleaning, or just hanging out at home might help you recall these experiences simply and passively. Listen to your favorite tunes has been found to reduce anxiety, lower blood pressure, increase sleep quality, and boost mood.

Make a habit of expressing appreciation regularly. It doesn't have to be a huge deal; simply make one to three simple comments each day such as, "I am glad for the roof over my head," "I am grateful for the light that rises each morning and feels on my skin," or "I am grateful for the wonderful strawberries I had today." Write in a diary or speak aloud the things you're grateful for at the end of each day, no matter how small they may be. Even in the most terrible or stressful situations, practicing thankfulness will help you put things into perspective, produce joy indirectly, and keep you grounded.

Spend time practicing your vision. Close your eyes and concentrate on your most cherished location, person, mantra, prayer, or even vacation. Inhale deeply and see yourself in this area or circumstance. Imagine the colors, flavors, textures, and dialogues. Spend five minutes immersed in the present moment, slowing your breathing and relaxing your body. Some folks find that laying down with bolsters under the legs and a weighted blanket on top of the torso or sitting in a chair with a cushion behind the back and under the feet makes this exercise more effective. Regularly practicing this type of meditation will help you remember that parts of whatever tough circumstance you're in, such as loneliness, grief, or desperation, are just transitory. You'll have more pleasant experiences again, and these little meditations may even assist you in creating new ones.

Every day, look for the "awe" moment. The idea of "awe" refers to a feeling of wonder and astonishment. Awe is usually associated with "big" experiences, such as diving the Great Barrier Reef or viewing the Eiffel Tower in Paris. Researchers are discovering, however, that we may enjoy the same advantages if we take the time to recognize little, joyful moments throughout the day. Seeing the sunrise or watching ants march, for example, may provide awe. Reading great poetry or going on a new trail and seeing intriguing rocks or flowers may also provide us with a sense of wonder. Take the time to notice things that you may have overlooked previously.

Finding out what brings you joy and happiness in life is the first step toward making yourself happy. This is evaluating the things that offer you joy rather than what social norms teach you about happiness. It's all too easy to get caught up in what you believe would make you happy rather than what truly makes you happy. People strive for the ideal relationship, the ideal home, the ideal body, and other people's approval to be happy. These things can make us joyful at times, but they can also cause us tension if we haven't achieved our goals or if we have and aren't satisfied. Other times, we are so focused on achieving a single goal that we don't have time for other aspects of our lives that would genuinely make us happy.

Have a Positive Attitude Towards Life

However, lifestyle is simply one factor in determining happiness. Your attitude toward life and the events that occur each day can have a significant influence on your overall happiness and life satisfaction.

It's certainly no surprise that optimists are happier, but you might not understand that optimism entails more than "putting on a cheerful face" or "looking on the bright side." Optimists have certain characteristics that help them achieve more achievements, better health, and greater life happiness.

Happy people have an internal center of control in addition to optimism. Simply defined, they feel they have control over their destiny rather than being victims of circumstance.

When you approach your life's difficulties as a challenge rather than a threat, you're more likely to find successful solutions. As you face these challenges, you also feel more energized rather than exhausted.

Many individuals strive for things they believe will make them happy, yet happiness isn't necessarily the outcome. We all know people who have poured their hearts and souls into their jobs, sacrificing their personal life in the process, only to wonder why they are successful but miserable.

It's also all too typical for people to have a gorgeous home, fancy cars, fashionable clothes, and often mountains of debt yet still feel less satisfied with their lives than they did before they had all these "things." So, how can you know which goals will satisfy you and which ones will not? You must strike a balance to make yourself happy. Solid work and financial security can help you be happy, but you must also consider other variables that contribute to happiness, such as your health, relationships, and other worthwhile hobbies. Remember all of the aspects of your life that are important to you when you create your objectives. Create a comprehensive description of how you want your entire life to appear, or establish monthly objectives and good habits for a single aspect of your life.

Many individuals sabotage themselves from the start by expecting too much and setting themselves up to fail, whether they are establishing objectives as New Year's resolutions or as part of a search for a better life. Many individuals, for example, expect to alter their behaviors overnight via sheer determination; any slip-ups are viewed as "failures," which all too frequently lead to the objective being abandoned and emotions of despair.

Self-Help for Happy Life

It's critical to set yourself up for success if you're attempting to make positive changes in your life!

Set small, realistic objectives first!

Work your way into a new habit in little increments, and you'll feel more accomplished and less inclined to give up along the way. Then, when you've made progress, reward yourself. Allow yourself to feel proud and even offer yourself a tiny reward for each minor objective you achieve. Don't forget to enlist the help of your friends and family. Tell the individuals who care about you what you're trying to accomplish and how successful you've been. This will offer you more strength and make giving up less tempting and have to explain yourself to those close to you.

While it is critical to explore long-term solutions to improve your happiness, there are also simple things you can do right now to improve your happiness. Here are a few examples:

Keep a Journal

Keeping a thankfulness diary is a good idea. According to research, having a higher sense of appreciation may lead to increased emotions of happiness. Participants in one research composed a daily appreciation list for 14 days and then reported increased levels of positive emotion, subjective pleasure, and life satisfaction.

Take a stroll around the neighborhood

Walking is a good strategy to improve mood in studies. Exercise may improve your mood and mental health on its own, but if you can, go for a walk outside to get the most out of it. Physical activity, time spent in nature, and exposure to sunlight can all help you feel happier.

Be amazed

People who feel awe have reduced stress levels and higher emotions of fulfillment, according to research. Staying interested in the world around you will help you have more awe-inspiring peak experiences.

Takeaway

We know that happiness predicts health and lifespan and that happiness measures may be used to assess societal development and policy effectiveness. Don't attempt to stop yourself from having bad ideas.

When you're feeling bad about yourself, think about what advice you'd offer a buddy who was feeling low. Now try to put that advice into practice in your life. The practice of confronting and correcting illogical beliefs is known as Socratic questioning. This approach has been shown in studies to help with depressive symptoms. There are many misconceptions regarding what would make you happy.

While being in a good, supportive love relationship helps, it's not true that you can't be happy and content if you're single. Singles with significant connections and hobbies are, in fact, happier than those in unsuitable love relationships. Play some of your favorite tunes. It can help you recollect happy experiences, giving you a break from the problems you're dealing with daily. Listen to music while working, cleaning, or just hanging out at home might help you recall these experiences simply and passively.

Finding out what brings you joy and happiness in life is the first step toward making yourself happy. This is evaluating the things that offer you joy rather than what social norms teach you about happiness. Many individuals strive for things they believe will make them happy, yet happiness isn't necessarily the outcome. Staying interested in the world around you will help you have more awe-inspiring peak experiences.

Chapter 10: Self-Help for Spiritual Care

Spirituality may mean different things to different individuals, and it's typically affected by the ideas you were exposed to as a child. Spirituality may conjure up images of religion or cultural traditions in your mind. Spiritual self-care in this context includes performing rituals, attending religious services or ceremonies, and studying religious literature.

Perhaps your definition of spirituality is found in nature, in others, or inside oneself. It might be via the mediums of art, music, or dance. In the end, it may be anything that is significant and instills a feeling of sanctity in you, even if you are the only one who feels it.

Spirituality is a matter of personal choice. Whatever road you choose, they all lead to something you want on some level: a sense of belonging, purpose, and pleasure.

Any ritual that links you to your actual self, the genuine you, is a spiritual self-care practice. The true self is the unadulterated manifestation of who you were born to be and what you have to give to the world. It's energetic, inspirational, and most importantly, it's comfortable. Maybe you've already experienced it, or maybe you've got a peek of how it may look or feel. Learning to recognize how you feel is a crucial aspect of being able to function in life.

What is The Significance of Spiritual Self-Care?

It is soul-satisfying to devote time to spiritual self-care. It promotes contemplation while also providing clarity and comfort. Various studies have demonstrated the numerous health advantages of having a spiritual life. A spiritual self-care practice quiets the mind and helps to soothe internal turmoil, allowing you to begin experiencing and respecting what your heart desires, as well as having the fortitude to make the required changes. Your body and emotions can't lie; you'll know deep down if you're genuinely happy and thriving. You have earned the right to live your life from this vantage point. Spiritual self-care can assist you in achieving the following goals:

- Enhance interpersonal ties and partnerships
- Feel more at ease inside yourself
- Get a better understanding of what makes you happy
- Boost emotions of unity and humanity
- Reduce emotions of loneliness and isolation

Here is a list of spiritual self-care exercises that everyone may start today

Contemplation

Contemplation is thinking about something continually, studying it, and reflecting on it, generally something good and essential in terms of life and meaning. The ego vanishes briefly when this sort of reflective activity gets very deep when a person becomes calm and very focused while pondering, and contemplation becomes progressively like meditation. At such times, solutions to life's difficulties might emerge unexpectedly.

Spend Time Outdoors

Spending time in nature is one of the most effective spiritual self-care activities we can engage in to attain maximum well-being. Spending time in nature decreases stress and is anti-inflammatory, according to research.

When individuals awaken or experience a profound spiritual transformation, they frequently feel compelled to spend more time in nature. While we open and clear our difficulties, a part of us yearns for a relationship devoid of ego and other garbage.

During the early stages of waking, some people remark about desiring a garden, relocating to a cabin in the woods, or anything like that. So, go ahead and give in to that need. Hikes should be taken. Spend some time at a lake or on a beach. It may be a fantastic way to refresh oneself.

Read a Book That Makes You Happy

One spiritual practice that can help us connect with our soul is reading an inspirational book.

"What excellent literature can and does do — far more than any importation of morality — is touch the human soul," Karen Swallow Prior has remarked.

Deep reading is a unique cognitive activity that helps us sympathize with others. As a result, it has the potential to make us smarter and nicer, among other things.

Meditation for Spiritual Care

Spiritual meditation is, at its root, the intentional practice of connecting to something bigger, faster, and deeper than oneself. It may seem counterintuitive, but the road to that connection is paved with honest self-reflection. While various meditation practices aim to improve spiritual awareness, they all necessitate an attitude of honesty and sincerity when it comes to how we see ourselves and the world. Meditation is practiced in various ways by many religions. Anyone may follow a guided spiritual meditation, and it is not confined to any specific faith or denomination.

We've relied on spiritual instructors' advice for as long as we've been starting on spiritual journeys. Wisdom, compassion, spiritual strength, and humility are all characteristics of a good spiritual teacher. Whether their intentions are good or bad, self-styled gurus who toot their own "spiritual enlightenment" horns tend to be misled and easily lead people astray. Meditation takes time to help you reach spiritual consciousness. Progress does not happen quickly, and claims of a rapid remedy are at best unrealistic. Spiritual enlightenment requires a great deal of dedication and effort, but the long-term advantages are immeasurable.

Keys to Successful Spiritual Meditation

The first stage is to learn everything there is to know about oneself. Like almost everyone else who commits to self-knowledge, you're likely to home in on aspects of yourself that you'd like to alter. The first step in really becoming friends with oneself is to acknowledge and accept who you are via spiritual meditation. In her book "Start Where You Are", meditation master PemaChödrön wonderfully states this: "It is unconditional compassion for ourselves that leads naturally to unconditional compassion for others." We shall be able to put ourselves in the shoes of others and never give up on them if we are ready to stand completely in our own shoes and never give up on ourselves.

Let Go of Whatever Grudges You've Been Harboring

Forgiving someone who has wronged you or someone you care about may be incredibly tough. However, as your spiritual meditation practice grows, you'll notice that carrying grudges brings you nothing but suffering and does nothing to assist others. The sooner you forgive, the easier it will be to let go of the sorrow and go on. Don't let an unwillingness to forgive get in the way of your spiritual awakening. By practicing mindfulness and hoping for the happiness of others, you may teach your mind to let go. It may take some time, but letting go is the apparent cure to clinging to resentment's anguish.

Focus Your Spiritual Aspirations on Others

True spirituality focuses on helping others, but in order to do so, we must first help ourselves. We learn to embrace who we are with love and generosity by looking at our own thinking. We may then share our sensitivity and generosity with others. We notice that the more we focus on the welfare of others, the less we worry about our own needs and disappointments as we continue our spiritual practice. We come to comprehend that we are all only attempting to be happy and that we are all attempting to avoid pain. We are all the same in this way.

Bring Mindfulness into Your Faith

Many people feel that exercising their faith is a tremendous source of comfort and spiritual nourishment. They find happiness at their meditation center or place of worship, or just by practicing with other people who share their interests.

Religious practices that preserve the basic spiritual foundations of kindness, openness, and connection can lead to spiritual awakening experiences that go beyond the commonplace.

Some people, on the other hand, use their faith to flee from life rather than accept it. You can stay open to the connection and rewards of the present moment by adding mindfulness into your spiritual practice.

Open Your Mind to New Possibilities

While we are all unique in many ways, there are certain common wants and experiences that all living things share. We all want to be happy and avoid pain, from the tiniest bug to the most powerful king. After all, none of us would be able to live without the help of others. The fact of our interconnection can be revealed via guided spiritual meditation, which can help us relativize our own value. Accepting that we're only a speck of cosmic dust in the cosmos, or a grain of sand, as some say, gives us a lot of freedom. We may open our thoughts to all the possibilities that this freedom offers us, rather than being locked in self-importance. Right now, we have the opportunity to embrace change and progress toward higher spiritual understanding.

Summary

This Book "Self-Help for Women of All Ages" is a complete guide on how to take care of yourself as a woman. It guides and highlights almost all aspects of life from trauma to divorce, from happiness to depression and anxiety, from addiction to career growth. In the first chapter, there is a brief introduction about self-help and what it means to women of all ages. In the upcoming chapters, self-help for mental health is highlighted. Our mental health is influenced by our emotional, psychological, and social well-being. It has an impact on the way we think, feel, and act. Your thinking, emotions, and behavior may be disrupted if you have mental health concerns at some point in your life.

Self-Help for depression says that depression and anxiety can affect a woman's life in a variety of ways. Women's physical health is being jeopardized, and they are feeling weak and destroyed. You're tired and sluggish.

Divorce is a difficult transition, especially for women. It's a chaotic period of financial and mental stress. It may appear simple and straightforward, but it is a major struggle that a woman must fight alone, facing all of life's challenges and defending herself against the never-ending questioning of those around her.

Taking care of oneself to be healthy should be the priority. Self-care entails taking proactive steps to improve one's physical, mental, and emotional well-being. Self-care can come in a variety of shapes and sizes. It might be as simple as getting adequate sleep each night or getting some fresh air for a few minutes.

A traumatized individual might feel a wide range of emotions, both in the immediate aftermath of the event and in the long run. For self-help in trauma, women should plan a get-together with old pals to spend quality time together. Throughout the day, eating small, well-balanced meals will help you retain your energy and reduce mood fluctuations.

Learning is a never-ending process. Never assume you know everything about anything in your life or job. There's always something new to discover. Continuous career progress occurs when you consistently increase your knowledge, abilities, experience, and efficiency.

Finding out what brings you joy and happiness in life is the first step toward making yourself happy. This is evaluating the things that offer you joy rather than what social norms teach you about happiness.

Don't miss out!

Visit the website below and you can sign up to receive emails whenever Dr. Robertino Bedenian publishes a new book. There's no charge and no obligation.

https://books2read.com/r/B-A-YQGQ-NGBTB

BOOKS 2 READ

Connecting independent readers to independent writers.

Also by Dr. Robertino Bedenian

Fitness Over 60 For Women – How to Stay Fit And Healthy As You Age
Does Back Pain Go Away? 10 Answers To The Most Acute Back Pain Issues
Massage Bible - A Beginners Guide To Western And Eastern Massage Therapy
Going Vegan - How To Vegan Without Going Crazy
Chiropraktik - Was Steckt Eigentlich Dahinter?
Massagen: Ein Überblick Über Westliche Und Östliche Massagetechniken
Natuerlich Abnehmen, Schlank Und Endlich Fit Sein
P.S. Ich Liebe Dich: Wenn Liebe So Einfach Wäre
Was Tun Bei Rückenschmerzen, Bandscheibenvorfall Und Ischiasschmerzen: 10 Antworten Zu Den Häufigsten Fragen Bei Rückenschmerzen
Was Tun Gegen Schlafapnoe, Schlafstörungen Und Schnarchen
Self-Help Books for Women
Diabetes How to Help: Everything You Need to Know About Diabetes Type 1 and Type 2
Diet and Workout Planner: How to Stay Healthy and Get Fit for Life
Everything I Know About Love
The Sleep Easy Solution Book: How to Stop Sleep Apnea, Snoring, and Sleep Disorders
Your Super Gut Feeling Restored – How to Restore Your Life Energy and Overall Health from The Inside Out

About the Author

Dr. Robertino Bedenian is a qualified fitness instructor accredited by the German Olympic Committee, a health and nutrition expert, and the author of several books on diet, health, and fitness!

For more than twenty years he has been a fitness coach at the sports university teaching aerobics, back gymnastics, stretching, high-intensity interval training (HIIT), power gymnastics, and athletic sports.

On his website, he has published more than 300 articles about the vegan lifestyle covering diet and health recommendations, detoxication programs,

fitness guidelines, and disease-related topics. He is part of a family with an orthopedic surgeon, a physical therapist, an osteopath, and an alternative practitioner.

He is also the founder of the brand "**Going Vegan**" selling high-quality supplements for optimal health.

You are more than welcome to check his website for more details:

https://goingveganhealthbenefits.com.

His brand has been awarded continuously with 5-star feedback by customers for its outstanding product quality.

Dr. Bedenian is also the founder of the book company "**Book Summary Publishing**" publishing summaries and workbooks of Amazon #1 bestselling non-fiction books.

If you want to learn more about the summaries and workbooks that he has published so far, please visit his website:

https://booksummarypublishing.com

Read more at https://booksummarypublishing.com.